WORLD ENERGY ISSUES

WATER POWER

Is It Efficient?

JIM PIPE

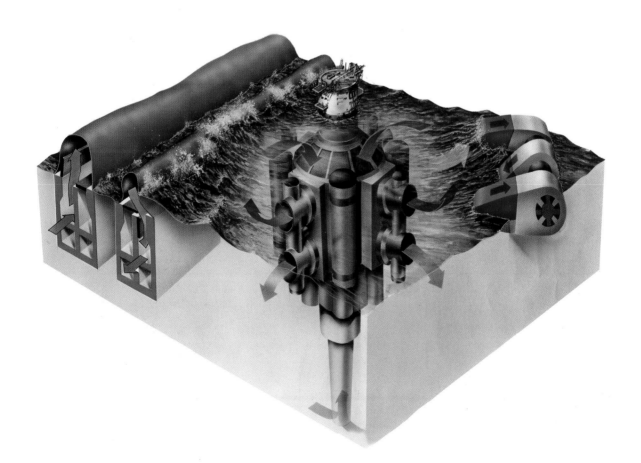

ALADDIN/WATTS
LONDON • SYDNEY

Contents

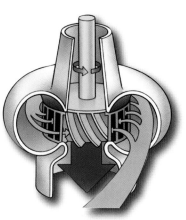

© Aladdin Books Ltd 2010

Designed and produced by
Aladdin Books Ltd
PO Box 53987
London SW15 2SF

First published in 2010
by Franklin Watts
338 Euston Road
London NW1 3BH

Franklin Watts Australia
Level 17/207 Kent Street
Sydney NSW 2000

Franklin Watts is a division of
Hachette Children's Books,
an Hachette UK company.
www.hachette.co.uk

All rights reserved
Printed in Malaysia

Scientific consultant: Rob Bowden

A catalogue record for
this book is available
from the British Library.

Dewey Classification:
333.9'14

ISBN 978 1 4451 0194 1

What's the Issue?

The power of flowing water has been used for centuries to grind grain and irrigate land. For over 100 years, it has also been used to create electricity. Today, it remains a major energy source, providing the power to work machines and to light or heat homes and offices. In countries such as Norway and Nepal, it supplies over 95 per cent of the electricity.

Water power may grow in importance as oil and gas become scarce. It is a clean, renewable energy source, unlike fossil fuels, which release gases that contribute to global warming. Though many of the best sites for hydroelectric power stations have been used, the latest technology may help us to harness the power of the oceans' waves and tidal currents, and to tap the heat energy stored in water deep underground.

⚉ Waterwheels
In the past, waterwheels used the power of flowing water to grind grain.

⚉ Mighty Hydropower
The Itaipu dam in Brazil is one of the world's largest hydroelectric power plants.

Why Water Power?

◐ Blue Planet

Over 70 per cent of the world's surface is covered in water – that's a lot of potential power waiting to be used.

Water power is the energy we get from flowing water – you can feel its power when you put your hand under a running tap. Using turbines, we can catch the energy from flowing water to make hydroelectricity. Hydroelectric power stations are expensive to build, but once they are up and running, they provide a cheap and reliable source of power.

Other machines have been built that capture the energy of flowing water in the oceans, whether waves crashing on a shore or the powerful currents created when the tide goes in and out. These are clean and renewable forms of energy – they don't pollute and they won't run out.

◐ The Water Cycle

Powered by the heat of the Sun, water moves in a never-ending cycle around our planet. Every time it rains, water flows down to the sea, a huge source of power just waiting to be tapped.

Water Energy – Five Ways To Use It

1 Trapping water behind a barrier or dam and using the stored energy to drive turbines, generating electricity.

2 Waves are created by wind blowing over water. The energy they contain can be tapped by machines.

3 As the Moon moves around the Earth, it tugs at the oceans, creating tides. This energy can also be turned into electricity.

4 The sea is warmer on the surface than at the bottom. This difference in temperature may be a future source of energy.

5 Some power plants catch the heat energy from hot water deep below the ground. These are called geothermal plants – from "geo" meaning ground and "thermal" meaning hot.

Wave energy

Wave currents

Wind

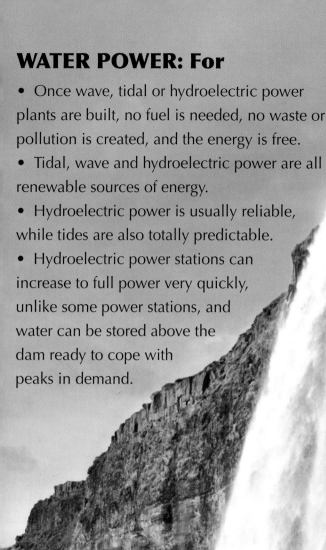

WATER POWER: For

• Once wave, tidal or hydroelectric power plants are built, no fuel is needed, no waste or pollution is created, and the energy is free.

• Tidal, wave and hydroelectric power are all renewable sources of energy.

• Hydroelectric power is usually reliable, while tides are also totally predictable.

• Hydroelectric power stations can increase to full power very quickly, unlike some power stations, and water can be stored above the dam ready to cope with peaks in demand.

WATER POWER: Against

• Wave power depends on the waves – only sites where waves are consistently strong all year are suitable.

• Wave and tidal machines must be tough enough to withstand very rough weather.

• Tidal power only operates for around 10 hours each day, when the tide is actually moving in or out. A tidal barrage is expensive to build and affects local water habitats. There are few suitable sites for tidal barrages.

• Dams are expensive to build and can flood very large areas, destroying habitats and forcing people to abandon their homes. Dams can also silt up or the water supply can dry up.

• Rotting vegetation in flooded valleys releases methane, a powerful greenhouse gas.

ENERGY FACTS: Global Water Power

• Water power provides about 20 per cent of the world's electricity. Most of this power comes from hydroelectric power stations.

• Hydroelectricity is the most common form of renewable energy. It accounts for over 80 per cent of electricity from renewable sources.

• China is the world's largest producer of hydroelectric power, followed by Canada, Brazil, the United States and Russia.

• Norway gets over 98 per cent of all its electricity from hydro-electric power stations.

What Is Water Power?

People have used water power, or hydropower, for thousands of years. Flowing water pushing against a large wheel was used to drive machinery inside a mill or factory, providing the energy to grind flour, weave cloth or saw timber. The main source of water power today comes from water flowing down rivers to the sea, especially in countries that have high mountains or steep valleys. These features cause the water to flow fast downhill, giving it lots of energy that can be turned into electricity by hydroelectric power stations.

◉ **Niagara Falls –** *Some of the falling water is diverted through channels to produce electricity.*

◑ Driven by Nature

Thanks to the force of gravity, rivers flow naturally downhill towards the sea. Water in the oceans is moved by the natural power of wind, currents and tides. All these different forms of energy can be used to produce mechanical or electrical power.

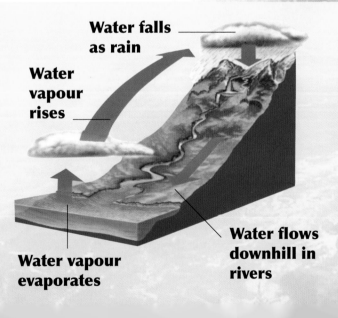

Water falls as rain

Water vapour rises

Water vapour evaporates

Water flows downhill in rivers

◔ The Water Cycle

The Sun's heat warms water in lakes and the oceans. This turns water into an invisible gas called water vapour, which rises up into the sky. Here the water vapour cools and turns back into drops of water. These fall back to the ground as rain or snow.

The rainwater flows into rivers down into the sea, where the whole process starts all over again. This is the water cycle. A cycle means something that goes around and around, which is exactly what happens to water on our planet.

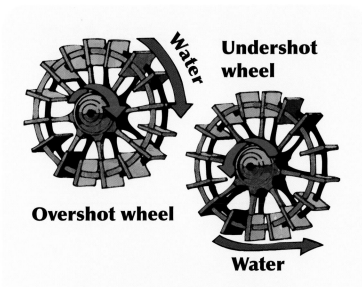

Undershot wheel

Water

Overshot wheel

Water

🜛 How a Waterwheel Works

1 *A waterwheel has buckets or paddles around the outside.*

2 *Water flows from a river or millpond along a trough to the wheel.*

3 *As the water flows, it fills the buckets or pushes against the paddles.*

4 *The force of the water makes the wheel turn.*

5 *The water then joins the river on the other side of the wheel.*

Early River and Wave Power

In medieval times, watermills were used to drive mechanical hammers and looms for making cloth. The power of a wave of water released from a tank was also used to extract metal ores, a process known as hushing. In China, "pot wheels" used the flow of the river to raise water to irrigate the fields.

Penstock

Mill

Water-wheel

🜛 Watermills

The flow of water onto the wheel was controlled by moving a lever which raised a sluice-gate just before the wheel. The gate that controlled the flow of water is called a penstock. The waterwheel was linked by a system of cogs and gears to machinery inside the mill, which ground wheat into flour.

7

Hydroelectric Power

In a hydroelectric power station, a dam is built across a river, trapping its water in an artificial lake, or reservoir. The water is allowed to flow down giant concrete tunnels, the penstocks, where it rushes into the dam's powerhouse. Here the force of the falling water pushes against the turbines' fins. When the turbines spin, the generators connected to them turn this movement into electricity. Dams can also be used as an energy store using a pumped storage system.

ⓥ How a Dam Works

Dams create a head of water. This is the energy of the water stored behind a dam. The higher the dam and the deeper the water stored behind it, the more energy it can produce. Dams use water power very efficiently, converting up to 90 per cent of its energy into electricity. They can also handle peaks in demand. When the demand for electricity is low, the dam simply stores more water (ready for use when demand is high).

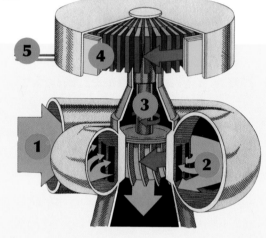

ⓐ How Electricity Is Generated

1 *Water under great pressure enters the turbine.*
2 *The water flows over the turbine blades.*
3 *This causes the turbine's shaft to turn.*
4 *At the top of the shaft are magnets that move through large coils of wire – the generator.*
5 *This generates electricity which then flows through power lines.*

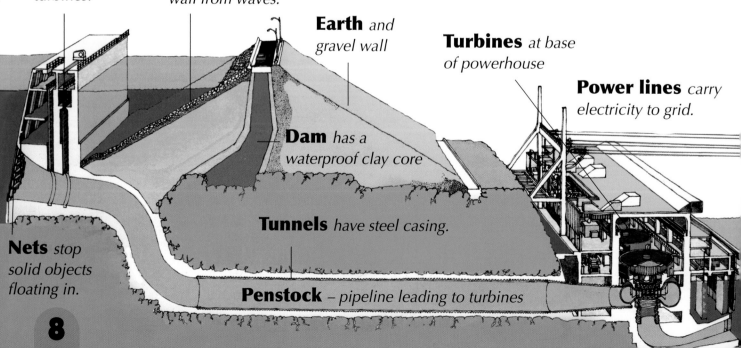

Sliding gates *control the water flowing to the turbines.*

Rip rap *rocks protect the dam wall from waves.*

Earth *and gravel wall*

Turbines *at base of powerhouse*

Power lines *carry electricity to grid.*

Dam *has a waterproof clay core*

Nets *stop solid objects floating in.*

Tunnels *have steel casing.*

Penstock *– pipeline leading to turbines*

▷ How Water Turbines Work

Turbines have curved blades that catch the flowing water – the faster the water flows, the faster they spin. Water is guided onto the turbines by channels and guide vanes.

In a large hydroelectric power station, the turbines are the size of a house.

Francis Turbine: *Water enters from the side, catching the fins.*

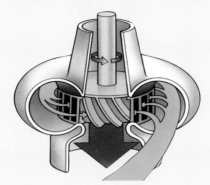

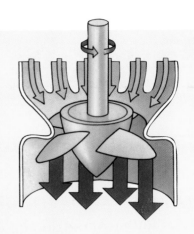

Propeller Turbine: *Water flows through the top of the turbine and down, spinning the turbine around.*

Upper reservoir

Water *is pumped up when demand is low.*

Water *flows down at peak demand.*

Lower reservoir

◁ Pumped Storage Plants

These hydroelectric power stations use the same water over and over. They consist of two reservoirs, one much higher than the other. When demand for electricity is high, water flows down from the upper reservoir through the powerhouse to create electricity. When demand is low, spare electricity in the grid is used to pump water back up to the higher reservoir.

The electricity generated by solar farms and wind turbines can also be stored by pumped storage plants in the same way.

▷ Building a Dam

Building a dam is a massive project that can take 10 or more years to finish. A large river may have to be diverted while the dam is being built. Dams are built using extremely thick walls of reinforced concrete. They must be completely watertight and strong enough to hold back the water in a full reservoir.

The Three Gorges Dam built on China's largest river, the Yangtse, is about 2,309 m long and 101 m high. Around 16 million tonnes of concrete were used to make the dam.

Dams in Action

In a large hydroelectric power station, the only sign of the water pounding through the powerhouse is the humming of the generators as they produce electricity.

The turbines work night and day, though the number working at any one time depends on the level of water or the demand for electricity. If the reservoir becomes too full and there is a danger of flooding, the extra water flows down a spillway, a channel at the side of the dam.

ENERGY FACTS: Dams

• The Grand Coulee Dam in the United States has 33 generators producing 6,800 MW of electricity, enough for 1.8 million people.
• When finished the Three Gorges Dam in China will have 32 main generators and will generate around 18,200 MW.
• The Itaipu dam in Brazil has 18 generators producing 12,600 MW, providing 25 per cent of Brazil's needs and more than 75 per cent of Paraguay's.

Dam wall

Penstock
Hydroelectric dams usually have several penstocks and a number of generators to produce the maximum amount of electricity.

Turbines
Water flowing down to the powerhouse is controlled by valves that work like giant taps.

◀) The Powerhouse

The turbines and generators are housed in the powerhouse. This building is often at the bottom of the dam and sometimes even in a giant cave in the rock beside the dam. Engineers keep an eye on everything from the control room. Computers automatically channel water through extra turbines when demand for electricity is high.

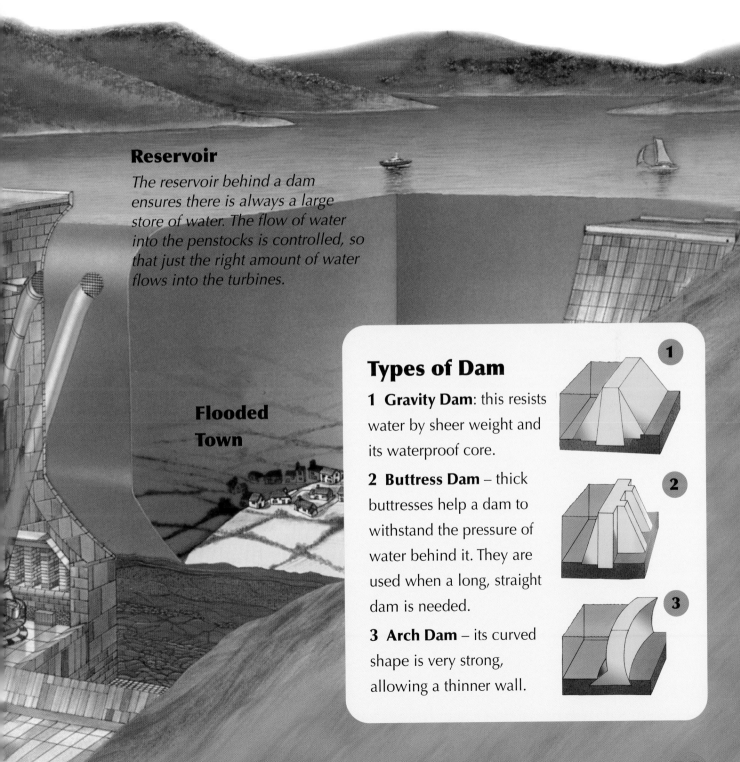

Reservoir

The reservoir behind a dam ensures there is always a large store of water. The flow of water into the penstocks is controlled, so that just the right amount of water flows into the turbines.

Flooded Town

Types of Dam

1 Gravity Dam: this resists water by sheer weight and its waterproof core.

2 Buttress Dam – thick buttresses help a dam to withstand the pressure of water behind it. They are used when a long, straight dam is needed.

3 Arch Dam – its curved shape is very strong, allowing a thinner wall.

Micro-Hydro

Smaller power plants, known as micro-hydro systems, can also produce electricity from flowing water. These are increasingly popular in remote areas such as in the Himalaya or Andes mountains, where small communities have to produce their own electricity. Many micro-hydro systems do not need a dam but use river water that flows into a pipe or trough. The water then flows through a small turbine connected to a generator. Other schemes simply place the turbine into a river.

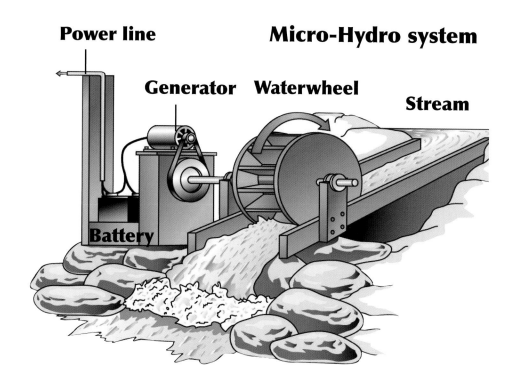

Power line **Micro-Hydro system**

Generator **Waterwheel**

Stream

Battery

◈ A Local Power Supply

Micro-hydro schemes can provide power for isolated farms and homes. These turbines are fitted with small waterwheels that can generate electricity efficiently even when the water flows at low speeds. They provide power for lights, fridges, tools and pumps.

Electricity from the generator can be stored in batteries in case the turbine breaks down. One of the big advantages of a micro-hydro system is that the electricity is produced very close to where it is being used. There is no need for large pylons and heavy transmission lines.

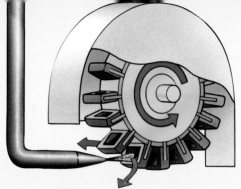

Peltron Wheel

Many smaller hydroelectric schemes have a turbine called a peltron wheel. This has a rim with cups or buckets to catch the water. A peltron wheel works well with a small stream flowing from a great height, such as a waterfall.

Connecting to the Grid

In theory, anyone with a river or stream at the end of their garden could use a micro-hydro system to generate their own electricity. More developed countries are also planning to install smart meters in homes. This will allow people with micro-hydro systems to sell on the extra electricity they produce when it has been raining heavily and the nearby river is flowing fast.

There is no need for batteries to store the electricity produced locally. Micro-hydro systems can be connected to the national grid, the network of power lines that supplies mains electricity to most homes.

⚡ Micro-hydro system in Nepal

Small-scale systems work well in less developed areas, especially where there is no other source of electricity.

⚡ Watermills of the Future

In Germany, many micro-hydro systems have been built where old watermills once stood.

Towards the Future

⚠ Fish Ladders

Some dams have a series of pools up the side called a fish ladder. The fish can pass by leaping or swimming up them. Sadly, many fish who don't make it up the ladder are injured or killed in the dam's turbines.

Hydroelectricity is by far the world's most important source of renewable energy. It is very reliable and though dams are costly to build, they provide cheap electricity. Big dams do flood large areas, however. They can destroy habitats and wildlife and force millions of people to abandon their homes. Recent research shows that dams may also add to global warming.

Newer forms of water power technology, using wave and tidal power, are renewable *and* clean, though they may also affect marine habitats if used on a large scale. Perhaps geothermal energy has the most potential if it can be tapped effectively in areas away from fault lines. All of these energy sources can work well when used locally.

A Fresh Water Store

The reservoirs behind dams can catch large amounts of water when it rains heavily, stopping areas downstream from being flooded. The fresh water can be piped to homes, factories and farms. But supplies are limited. Water levels in Lake Mead, the reservoir behind the Hoover Dam in Nevada, USA, have dropped 50 per cent in ten years due to rising demand from cities such as Las Vegas. If the lake goes dry, there'll be no more fresh water – and no electricity.

◖ Future Potential

Today, there are hydropower projects being built in some 80 countries. China, India, Iran and Turkey are all building large-scale hydroelectric plants while less developed countries such as Sudan, Mali, Cuba, Myanmar and Armenia all see hydropower as a vital source of future energy for homes and industry.

White Water

If dammed, the Inga Rapids in the Democratic Republic of Congo could provide enough electricity to meet all of Africa's current electricity needs.

◑ A Cause of Pollution

When a new dam is built, it can flood large areas of vegetation. As the flooded plants begin to rot, they produce significant amounts of carbon dioxide and methane. Dams in tropical areas, such as the Curuá-Una dam in Brazil, may have produced more greenhouse gases than an equivalent power plant burning fossil fuels.

Wave Power *Just 0.2 percent of the energy in ocean waves could power the entire planet – the tough part is finding a cheap way to turn this power into usable energy.*

◑ **Pelamis**
wave generator being tested at sea.

Tidal Power

We can also harness the flow of water in rising and falling tides. Dams built across estuaries are called barrages. There are barrages in France, Canada and Russia and a giant barrage is planned across the Severn Estuary off the west coast of England.

There are also several projects to build tidal machines that work like wind turbines. In 2008, a 1.2 MW tidal turbine went into operation in Northern Ireland and there are plans to build a huge tidal power field off the South Korean coast, with 300 18 m-high tidal 1 MW turbines sitting on the sea floor.

◔ Tidal Barrage

Bays or river mouths are the best place to build tidal power stations. As the tide rises, the water flows through the dam, generating power as it flows past turbines. At high tide, the sluice gates shut and the water is trapped.

As the tide drops, water is allowed to flow through the barrage, again turning the turbines, which can operate in both directions.

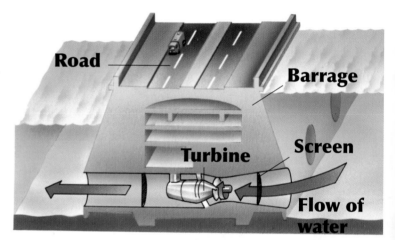

Road · Barrage · Turbine · Screen · Flow of water

⬡ Rance Barrage – *The first working tidal barrage was built in 1966 on the River Rance in northern France. The dam is 700m long and its 24 turbines produce some 240 MW of electricity, about a quarter as much as a coal-fired power station.*

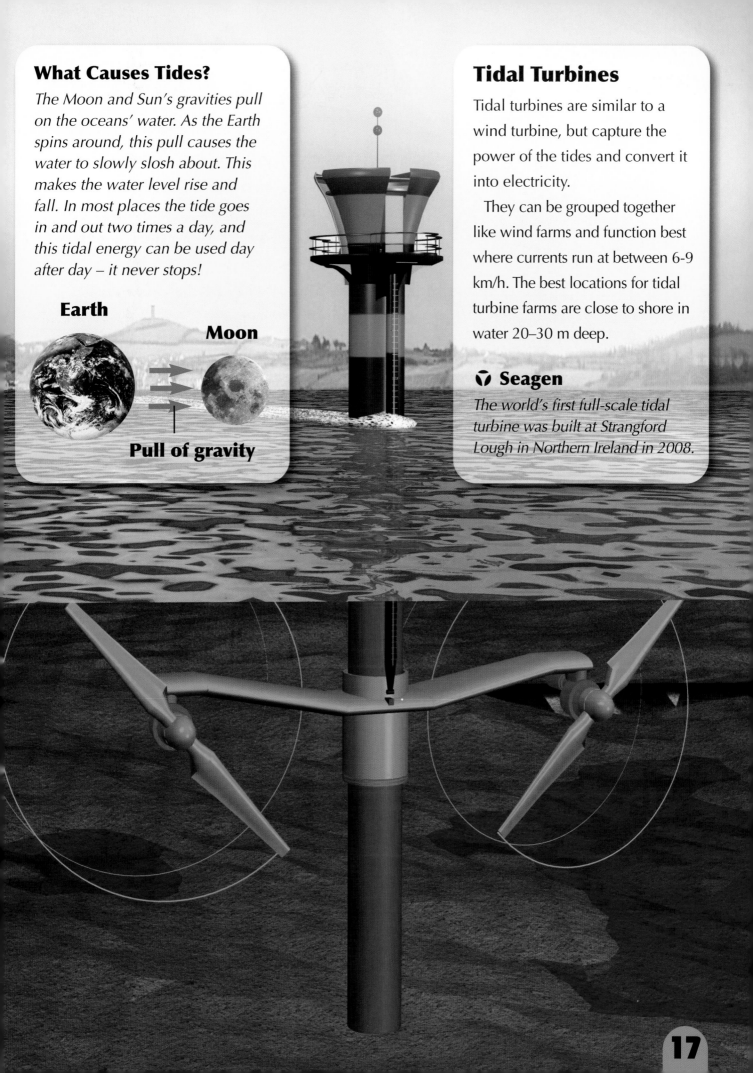

What Causes Tides?

The Moon and Sun's gravities pull on the oceans' water. As the Earth spins around, this pull causes the water to slowly slosh about. This makes the water level rise and fall. In most places the tide goes in and out two times a day, and this tidal energy can be used day after day – it never stops!

Earth

Moon

Pull of gravity

Tidal Turbines

Tidal turbines are similar to a wind turbine, but capture the power of the tides and convert it into electricity.

They can be grouped together like wind farms and function best where currents run at between 6-9 km/h. The best locations for tidal turbine farms are close to shore in water 20–30 m deep.

❦ Seagen

The world's first full-scale tidal turbine was built at Strangford Lough in Northern Ireland in 2008.

Shaft *joined to turbine*

Wave motion

◑ Nodding Ducks

This system uses floats fixed to a central shaft. The motion of waves drives hydraulic pumps inside the floats, turning a shaft connected to a turbine. The floats get their name from their bird-like profile and the way they bob up and down in the water.

Wave Power

When the wind blows across the sea, it creates waves. The stronger the wind, the bigger the wave. A wave machine can catch this energy and convert it to electricity. Experimental wave power plants have been built in many countries, including the UK, Japan, Australia and Norway, and in 2008 the world's first wave farm was built off the coast of Portugal.

Some wave power stations are built along the coast, using the power of waves as they crash onto the shore. Other wave machines float on the water. As they bob up and down, they move hydraulic pumps that are connected to a turbine.

◑ Coastal Wave Power

Wave power stations can be built along the seashore. As waves crash onto the shore, they force air in and out of a long tube inside the power station, spinning a turbine and generating electricity. A power station of this sort, named the Limpet, is operating on the Scottish island of Islay.

Limpet

◑ How It Works

1 *Waves rush into the Limpet power station.*
2 *The waves make the water rise and fall inside the power station.*
3 *The moving water forces the air back and forth through a tube at the top of the station.*
4 *A turbine in this tube is turned by the air rushing in and out. This is connected to a generator.*

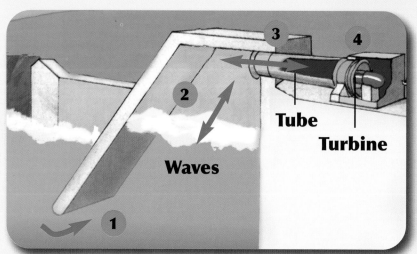

Waves

Tube

Turbine

▼ Floating Wave Power

Some wave generators float on the sea, with hinged joints that bend up and down as waves pass by. This motion works pumps that turn a turbine. The Pelamis system is named after a sea snake due to its shape – it's 120 m long and 3.5 m wide. The electricity flows down a cable along the seabed to the shore. A farm of Pelamis wave machines covering 1 km² of ocean could provide electricity for 20,000 homes in a country like the UK.

Pelamis

OCEAN POWER DELIVERY LTD

Aquabuoy

▶ Water Pistons

Some wave machines don't need to face the waves. Instead they can absorb the energy from waves coming in any direction. One device, the Aquabuoy, is a vertical tube below the water.

When waves rush in, they drive a sort of piston – a buoyant disc – up and down. As it moves, the disc pumps the water up hoses, turning a built-in turbine connected to an electrical generator. A group of buoys is connected to shore by an electrical cable.

Rainwater
Geyser
Cold water trickles down
Steam rises up
Molten Rocks

Heat Energy

So far we have looked at the power of flowing water. Geothermal, or "hot earth" energy, taps the energy from hot water deep below the Earth's surface. Hot molten rocks heat up the water, some of which travels upwards through cracks and appears on the surface as hot springs or geysers. By drilling wells into underground reservoirs, we can pump the hot water and steam to the surface. This can be used to generate electricity by blasting the steam against a turbine.

Heat from the Earth's Core

Geothermal energy is generated in the Earth's core, where temperatures of 7000 °C are produced – hotter than the Sun's surface! This heat flows outward and transfers to the surrounding layer of rock, the mantle. Some mantle rock melts, becoming magma, and this slowly moves up towards the Earth's crust. Here the magma heats nearby rock and water, creating a natural reservoir of very hot water.

⬤ Rising Steam

Hot springs and geysers occur naturally. Cold rainwater seeps into the Earth's crust. Molten rocks heat the water up and it rises again as steam.

◖ Power Plant

At Nesjavellir in Iceland, hot water rises to the surface, forming hot springs. The geothermal power station built here in 1990 produces 120 MW of power (enough for over 80,000 homes) and provides around 1,800 litres of hot water a second to Iceland's capital, Reykjavik.

▼ Fault Lines

The Earth's crust is broken into giant pieces called plates. Magma comes close to the Earth's surface near the edges of these plates in areas known as fault lines. This is where volcanoes and earthquakes often occur. In the past, most geothermal power plants were built above fault lines as magma was relatively close to the surface.

World's Major Fault Lines

Hot Spots

Rock scientists called geologists do a lot of exploring to locate underground areas that contain pools of geothermal water. Test wells are drilled using special equipment that can cope with very high temperatures and cut through hard rock. A good geothermal site needs:

- Soft rocks that store water underground.
- A solid cap rock to trap the water and steam, such as clay.
- A heat source, such as magma.

▼ Hot Springs

Boiling mud pools, hot springs, geysers and volcanic vents can all point towards a possible site for a geothermal power station. Hot springs like the one below also provide a relaxing warm bath!

Geothermal Power

Until recently, there were two types of geothermal power plant. A dry steam reservoir produces steam but very little water. The steam is pumped directly into the power plant and provides the force that spins the turbines. In a hot water reservoir, water at 200-370 °C is brought up to the surface. Here it turns, or "flashes", into steam that is piped to the turbines. However, a new type of geothermal power plant can run on water that isn't as hot, so it doesn't need to be built above a fault line.

◖ Thermal Pool

Hot springs can also be used to generate heat. In Iceland, houses are heated by hot water pumped from the ground.

◗ Steam Power

A geothermal power station in Krafla, Iceland

A New Breed of Geothermal

Unlike countries such as Iceland, Italy or Indonesia, Germany does not have volcanic activity or dry steam reservoirs that can be used to produce electricity directly. In recent years, however, several plants have opened thanks to a new technology. A simple pipe going 3-4 km deep into the Earth taps a reservoir of water at 160 °C. This hot water is pumped up the pipe into a heat exchanger. Here it heats up another liquid, turning it into gas, and it's this gas that drives the turbines that produce electricity. The hot water also provides heating for homes nearby.

Geothermal Power Plant

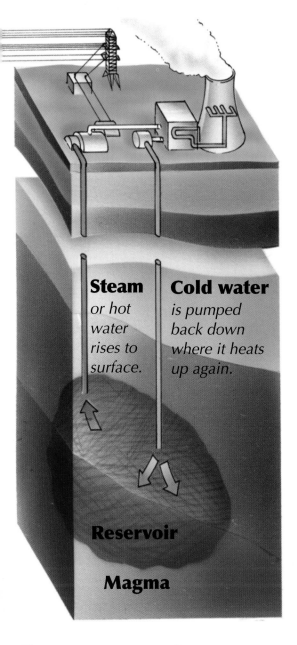

Steam *or hot water rises to surface.*

Cold water *is pumped back down where it heats up again.*

Reservoir

Magma

Geothermal Advantages

• **Clean**. Geothermal plants do give off water vapour, a major greenhouse gas, but they do not emit toxic gases.
• **Small**. Geothermal power needs less land per megawatt than almost any other power plant.
• **Reliable.** Geothermal power plants can run 24 hours a day, all year, and a geothermal power plant sits right on top of its fuel source.
• **Flexible**. The latest geothermal plants can be built anywhere, even in remote locations that are not connected to a national grid by power lines.

▷ Hot Dry Rocks

A new way of using geothermal energy is now being explored by scientists. Cold water is pumped down 6-km deep holes drilled in the dry rock. Here it is heated by hot rock layers then pumped back to the surface to create electricity and heat.

This Enhanced Geothermal System (EGS) can be drilled anywhere in the world as it does not require underground reservoirs of hot water or steam.

EGS *test plant at Soultz in France*

New Technology

If the hydroelectric power from a single river like the Yangtse can provide electricity for millions of homes, then imagine the untapped energy of the world's waves and tidal currents. Today, scientists are also looking at ways to exploit the heat energy stored in the oceans, especially in warm waters near the Equator.

While other renewables such as wind and solar power have been widely adopted in recent years, wave and tidal energy have been slow to take off. But if we can get the technology right, water power could meet an important part of the world's future energy needs – without adding to global warming.

Kite Power

The Deep Green project is a plan to sink underwater kites in British waters, to harness the power of ocean currents. Each kite would weigh around 7 tonnes and produce 0.5 MW of electricity, enough for 300 or more homes.

Wing

Turbine

Tether

Electric Cables

How the Kites Work

The kites are attached to the ocean bed with a tether and they can be controlled with a rudder so they point in the right direction. The kite-like wings help to increase the speed of the water as it flows over them and into the underwater turbine.

☀ Thermal Giants – OTEC

The ocean's surface traps heat from the Sun but deeper parts of the sea are cooler: the difference is about 20 °C in tropical regions. Scientists have found a way to use these temperature changes to turn liquid ammonia into gas. The gas expands, driving turbines that generate electricity. This process is known as Ocean Thermal Energy Conversion (OTEC).

If it is ever built, a 500 m-tall OTEC system could offer a cheap source of electricity, but if it pumps warm water into the lower layers of the sea it could damage sealife.

Tidal Lagoons

Tidal lagoons are built from rock and rubble around the shallow waters of a bay. Like barrages, they harness the power of tidal currents, but they're cheaper to build and have less impact on the environment. They can also be set up to generate power continuously. Tests for a possible barrage are now being carried out in Swansea Bay, Wales.

☀ How OTEC Works

1 *Warm water is pumped in at the top.*
2 *Warm water turns liquid ammonia into gas.*
3 *Warm water is pumped out.*
4 *Cold water is sucked up from the deep and cools the ammonia gas, turning it back to liquid.*
5 *Cold water is pumped out.*

◄ Working with Wind Power

Wave Treader machines are mounted on the base of offshore wind turbines. In the right weather, each machine could generate almost 0.5 MW, enough to power 300 homes in the UK.

As waves ripple past the wave power machine, they move arms either side of the wind turbine. These push against cylinders that contain hydraulic fluid, spinning a hydraulic motor. This in turn drives an electric generator. The electricity is then transmitted back to shore along the cable shared with the wind turbine. A Wave Treader can turn to face whichever way the wind is blowing.

HOT OFF THE PRESS

Wind Turbines Linked to Dams

■ A new energy initiative known as the *Spirit of Ireland* plans to reduce Ireland's dependence on fossil fuels by linking a large grid of wind turbines to a number of new pumped storage reservoirs. Wind turbines off the west coast, one of the windiest places in Europe, will generate the electricity. Some of this will then be used to pump sea water into storage reservoirs. When the wind isn't blowing, the dam releases the water, providing a reliable power source 24 hours a day.

Water mains

Sewage Power

■ In some towns in the United States, hydroelectric generators are already used in the water mains to produce electricity that can be used locally. Another scheme proposes placing water turbines in sewers, using the power of the flowing waste to generate electricity.

The many ice-sculpted valleys that run down to the Atlantic on the west coast of Ireland are a perfect site for storage reservoirs.

Renewable Energy "Supergrid"

■ Nine European countries are planning to link their clean energy projects around the North Sea. Thousands of kilometres of undersea cables will connect giant solar farms in Germany with wind turbines off Scotland and wave machines off the Dutch coast.

This renewables supergrid could supply electricity across the continent wherever the wind is blowing, the Sun is shining or the waves are crashing.

Hydroelectric power stations in Norway will also allow the renewables to store electricity when demand is low, in the form of pumped water storage.

One for the Buoys

■ In November 2009, work started on the Wave Hub project off the coast of Cornwall in the south-west UK. Based some 16 km off the north coast of Cornwall, this will feature a large grid-connected "socket" on the seabed that will allow up to four different marine energy devices to connect to it at any one time. Companies will then be able to test the devices for several years without extra permits.

Several firms are developing wave machines that use a system of "smart" ocean-going buoys to capture and convert wave energy into low-cost, clean electricity. A 10 MW wave power station (providing enough electricity for 6,000 homes) would cover just over 0.1 km^2 of sea.

The PowerBuoy wave machine

Dam Causes Pollution and Landslides

■ Around 1.2 million people were forced to leave their homes when the Three Gorges Dam in China was first built, as it flooded large areas with a new reservoir the same length as Britain.

Recently, engineers have also found that the giant dam is creating dangerous landslides and water pollution due to the rise and fall of such a large amount of water. The problem is so bad that another 300,000 people may be forced to move from their homes for their own safety.

World's Largest Wave Machine

■ A 315 kW Oyster, the world's largest hydroelectric wave machine, was joined to the UK national electricity grid in November 2009. It is now undergoing sea trials. These will be used to develop Oyster 2, in which three linked devices will generate 2.5 MW of power.

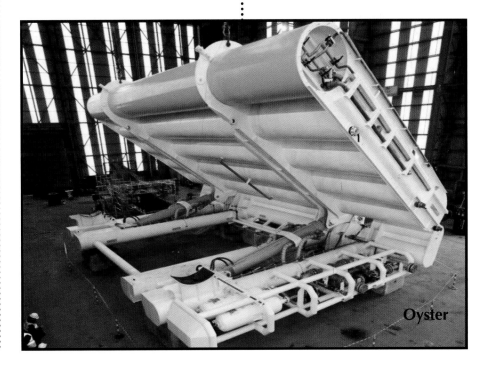

Oyster

How Water Compares

While fossil fuels are cheap, they release carbon dioxide into the atmosphere, causing pollution and global warming. Water power and other forms of renewable energy will reduce this problem, but may only be able to supply 20 per cent of our energy needs. Nuclear power could provide us with the extra power, but reactors are very expensive and take years to build.

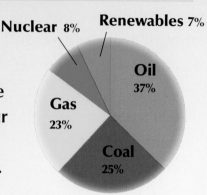

World Energy Sources

Nuclear 8% Renewables 7% Oil 37% Gas 23% Coal 25%

NON-RENEWABLE ENERGY

Oil

For:
Oil is cheap and easy to store, transport and use.

Against:
Oil is not renewable and it is getting more expensive to get out of the ground. Burning oil releases large amounts of greenhouse gases. Oil spills, especially at sea, cause severe pollution.

Gas

For:
Gas is relatively cheap, and produces less greenhouses gases than oil and coal.

Against:
Burning gas releases carbon dioxide. Gas is not renewable and the world's natural gas reserves are limited. Gas pipelines can disrupt the migration routes of animals such as caribou.

Coal

For:
Coal is cheap and supplies of coal are expected to last another 150 years.

Against:
Coal-fired power stations give off the most greenhouse gases. They also produce sulphur dioxide, creating acid rain. Coal mining can be very destructive to the landscape.

Nuclear

For:
Nuclear power is constant and reliable, and doesn't contribute to global warming.

Against:
Not renewable as uranium (the main nuclear fuel) will eventually run out. Nuclear waste is so dangerous it must be buried for thousands of years. Also the risk of a nuclear accident.

Hydroelectric Power

For:
Hydroelectric power needs no fuel, is renewable and doesn't pollute.

Against:
Hydro-electric is very expensive to build. A big dam floods a very large area upstream, impacting on animals and people there. The flooded areas give off methane, a greenhouse gas.

Tidal Power

For:
Tidal power needs no fuel, is reliable, renewable and doesn't pollute.

Against:
Tidal power machines are expensive to build and only provide power for around 10 hours each day, when the tide is actually moving in or out. Not an efficient way of producing electricity.

Geothermal Power

For:
Geothermal power needs no fuel, it's renewable and doesn't pollute.

Against:
There aren't many suitable places for a geothermal power station as you need hot rocks of the right type and not too deep. It can "run out of steam". Underground poisonous gases can be a danger.

Wind Power

For:
Wind power needs no fuel, it's renewable and doesn't pollute.

Against:
Wind is unpredictable, so wind farms need a back-up power supply. Possible danger to bird flocks. It takes thousands of wind turbines to produce the same power as a nuclear plant.

Biofuels

For:
Biofuels are cheap and renewable and can be made from waste.

Against:
Growing biofuels from energy crops reduces the land available for food and uses up vital resources such as fresh water. Like fossil fuels, biofuels can produce greenhouse gases.

Solar Power

For:
Solar power needs no fuel, it's renewable and doesn't pollute.

Against:
Solar farms using PV cells are still relatively expensive – they cost a lot to make compared to the amount of electricity they produce. They're unreliable unless used in a very sunny climate.

Glossary and Resources

barrage A dam built across an estuary.

climate The average weather in a region over a long period of time.

fish ladder A series of step-like pools that allow fish to move upstream past a dam.

flash When superhot water at high pressure below the ground reaches the surface, the low pressure here turns it to steam.

fossil fuel A fuel such as coal, oil or gas that is formed underground from the remains of prehistoric plants and animals.

generator A machine that turns the energy of a moving object into electricity.

geothermal power Power extracted from heat stored below the Earth's surface.

global warming A warming of the Earth's surface. Many scientists predict that global warming may lead to more floods, droughts and rising sea levels.

greenhouse effect The global warming caused by human-made gases, such as carbon dioxide and methane, that trap the heat from the Sun in the atmosphere.

heat exchanger A device that transfers heat from one substance to another.

hydroelectricity Electricity produced by flowing water, especially from dams built to create a reservoir.

hydropower Another term for hydroelectricity.

megawatt (MW) A million watts (a watt is a unit of power). A gigawatt is 1,000 MW.

micro-hydro A small system for producing hydroelectricity.

national grid A country's network of electric power lines.

penstock A valve, gate or pipeline that controls the rate of water flow to a water mill or the turbines in a hydroelectric dam.

powerhouse The building near a dam that houses the turbines and generators.

power station A plant where electricity is generated.

pumped storage A way of storing electricity by pumping water to a high reservoir, then letting it flow back down past turbines when demand is high.

pylon A tall metal tower that supports high voltage electric cables.

renewable Something that can be used over and over without running out.

reservoir A lake created behind a dam.

spillway A channel or passage that carries excess water over or around a dam to stop it from being damaged.

tidal range The difference in height between the highest and lowest tides in a particular place.

turbine A machine with rotating blades.

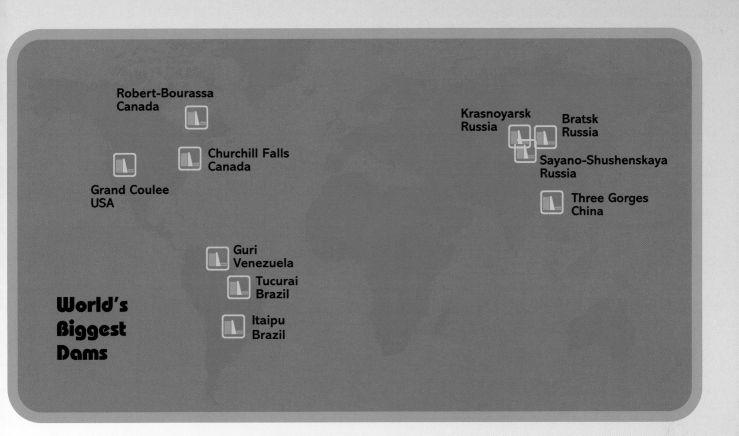

World's Biggest Dams

Robert-Bourassa
Canada

Churchill Falls
Canada

Grand Coulee
USA

Guri
Venezuela

Tucurai
Brazil

Itaipu
Brazil

Krasnoyarsk
Russia

Bratsk
Russia

Sayano-Shushenskaya
Russia

Three Gorges
China

Useful Websites

If you're interested in finding out more about water power, the following websites are helpful:

www.therenewableenergycentre.co.uk
www.fwee.org
www.tonto.eia.doe.gov/kids
www.darvill.clara.net/altenerg/hydro.htm
www.kids.esdb.bg/ocean.html
www.science.howstuffworks.com/wave-energy.htm

ENERGY FACTS:
Top 10 Hydroelectric Nations

Countries with the most hydropower in 2009 (power given in megawatts):

1 **China** – 171,520 MW
2 **Canada** – 88,970 MW
3 **United States** –79,500 MW
4 **Brazil** – 69,080 MW
5 **Russia** – 45,000 MW
6 **India** – 33,600 MW
7 **Norway** – 27,528 MW
8 **Japan** – 27,229 MW
9 **Sweden** – 16,209 MW
10 **France** – 15,335 MW

Further Reading

World Issues: Energy Crisis by Ewan McLeish (Aladdin/Franklin Watts)
Our World: Water Power by Chris Oxlade (Aladdin/Franklin Watts)
Energy Sources: Water Power by Neil Morris (Franklin Watts)
Energy Debate: Water Power by Richard and Louise Spilsbury (Wayland)
Energy in Action: Water Power by Ian F. Mahaney (PowerKids Press)
Issues in Our World: Energy Crisis by Ewan McLeish (Aladdin/Franklin Watts)

Index

Photocredits

(Abbreviations: t – top, m – middle, b – bottom, l – left, r – right).

All photos istockphoto.com except: 3b, 9br: Itaipu. 4tl: Stockbyte. 11tl, 26: US Department of Energy. 12-13: Courtesy IT Power. 14bl: Angelo Turconi. 15b, 19t: Pelamis Wave Power. 17: Sea Generation Ltd. 18mr: Wavegen. 19br: Finavera Renewables. 23br: Courtesy Géothermie Soultz. 24: Courtesy Minesto AB. 25bl: Courtesy Green Ocean Energy Ltd. 27 mt: Courtesy Ocean Power Technologies. 27 br: Courtesy Aquamarine Power.